MY SCIENCE
INVESTIGATIONS

Experiments with PLANTS

Christine Taylor-Butler

Heinemann
LIBRARY
Chicago, Illinois

H www.heinemannraintree.com
Visit our website to find out more information about Heinemann-Raintree books.

To order:

☎ Phone 888-454-2279

💻 Visit www.heinemannraintree.com to browse our catalog and order online.

Edited by Rebecca Rissman, Dan Nunn, and Catherine Veitch
Designed by Richard Parker
Picture research by Tracy Cummins
Originated by Capstone Global Library
Printed and bound in China

15 14 13
10 9 8 7 6 5 4 3

Library of Congress Cataloging-in-Publication Data
Taylor-Butler, Christine.
  Experiments with plants / Christine Taylor-Butler.—1st ed.
    p. cm.—(My science investigations)
  Includes bibliographical references and index.
  ISBN 978-1-4329-5362-1 (hc)—ISBN 978-1-4329-5368-3
(pb) 1. Plants—Experiments—Juvenile literature. 2. Science projects—Juvenile literature. I. Title.
  QK52.6.T39 2012
  580.78—dc22   2010042653

Acknowledgments
We would like to thank the following for permission to reproduce photographs: Getty Images p. 7 (Noel Hendrickson/Blend Images); Heinemann Raintree pp. 8, 9, 10, 12, 13, 14, 16, 17, 18, 19, 20, 21, 24, 25, 26 (Karon Dubke); National Geographic Stock p. 29 (© Martha Cooper); Shutterstock pp. 4 (© Dr. Morley Read), 5 (© WellyWelly), 27 (© Le Do), 28 (© Morgan Lane Photography).

Cover photograph of a boy experimenting on a plant reproduced with permission of Photolibrary (Imagesource Imagesource). Background photograph of a leaf surface reproduced with permission of istock photo (© Jarek Szymanski).

Special thanks to Suzy Gazlay for her invaluable help in the preparation of this book. We would also like to thank Ashley Wolinski for her help in the preparation of this book.

Disclaimer
All the Internet addresses (URLs) given in this book were valid at the time of going to press. However, due to the dynamic nature of the Internet, some addresses may have changed, or sites may have changed or ceased to exist since publication. While the author and publisher regret any inconvenience this may cause readers, no responsibility for any such changes can be accepted by either the author or the publisher.

Contents

Some words are printed in bold, **like this**.
You can find out what they mean by looking
in the Glossary.

Incredible Plants

Plants need sunlight, water, and a place to grow.

Plants are important to humans. They provide us with food and **materials** for shelter. Many medicines are made from plants. Your clothes may have been made from plants.

Redwood trees can grow as tall as a 30-story building!

Scientists who study plants are called **botanists**. They have found more than 400,000 kinds of plants in the world. Many of these plants grow in rain forests. The biggest plants are redwood trees. Redwood trees can grow to more than 300 feet tall!

How Scientists Work

Scientists start with a question about something they **observe**, or notice. They gather information and think about it. Then they make a guess, or **hypothesis**, about a likely answer to their question. Next they set up an **experiment** to test their hypothesis. They look at the **data**, or **results**, and make a decision, or **conclusion**, about whether their hypothesis is right or wrong. Either way, the scientists learn something!

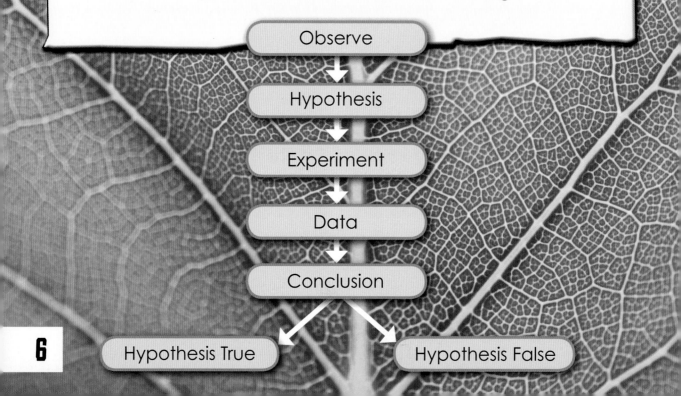

Observe

↓

Hypothesis

↓

Experiment

↓

Data

↓

Conclusion

Hypothesis True   Hypothesis False

How To Do an Experiment

1. Start a **log**. Write down your **observations**, question, and hypothesis.
2. Plan step-by-step how you can test your hypothesis. This is called the **procedure**.
3. Carry out the experiment. **Record** everything that happens. These are your observations.
4. Compare your results with your hypothesis. Was your hypothesis right or wrong? What did you learn? The answer is your conclusion.

Lima Beanstalk

In the fairy tale *Jack and the Beanstalk*, a giant beanstalk grows from a bean. A bean is a **seed**. How can a bean grow into a beanstalk? A seed contains everything needed to form a new plant. All it needs is water, light, and a place to grow.

Hypothesis

A seed will grow if it has water and sunlight, even if it isn't planted in soil.

You will need these things for the **experiment**.

Procedure

1. Soak three lima beans in water overnight.
2. In the morning, soak a paper towel with water. Squeeze out some of the water.
3. Fold the paper towel. Place the lima beans inside the towel.
4. Place the paper towel inside a plastic sandwich bag.

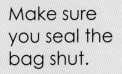

Make sure you seal the bag shut.

5. Place the bag on a sunny window ledge.
6. After 24 hours, look inside the bag. Have the beans changed?
7. Repeat step 6 for at least five days, or until your **seeds sprout** and grow. If the towel begins to dry out, add a teaspoon of water.

Record your **observations** in a **log**.

8. Each day look at the seeds and **record** what you see in a chart like the one below.

The science explained

The plastic bag provides a safe place for the seeds to sprout. After a while, the seeds will need to be planted in soil to continue growing.

	day 1	day 2	day 3	day 4	day 5
seeds	≈≈≈	≈≈≈	≈≈≈	≈≈≈	≈≈≈

Use your log to write or draw what you **observe** in a chart like this.

Up It Goes!

Plants need water to grow and stay alive. They take in water through their **roots**. Water also keeps cut flowers alive. How do cut flowers take in water if they have no roots? Do this **experiment** to find out.

Hypothesis

A plant will take in water even if it has no roots.

Warning!

You will need these **materials** and a ruler for the experiment. Be careful with sharp knives.

Procedure

1. Half fill a glass with water. Add ten drops of food color to the glass. Mix well.
2. Ask an adult to help you carefully cut off the end of a celery stick. Place the stick in the glass.
3. Check the celery every hour. Has the color moved up the stick? Measure the color from the bottom of the stick. **Record** your **observations**.

4. After two to three days, ask an adult to help you cut a slice as wide as your finger from the bottom of the stick. What can you see if you look at it with a magnifying glass? Draw it in your **log**.

The Science Explained

Plant **stems** have special tubes that take in water. The dots of color in your celery stick show you where the tubes are.

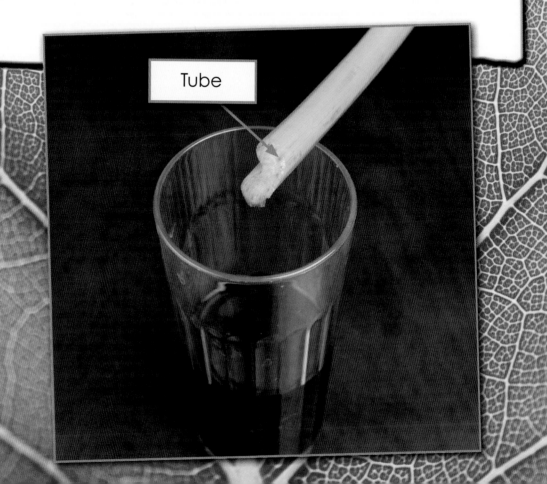

Tube

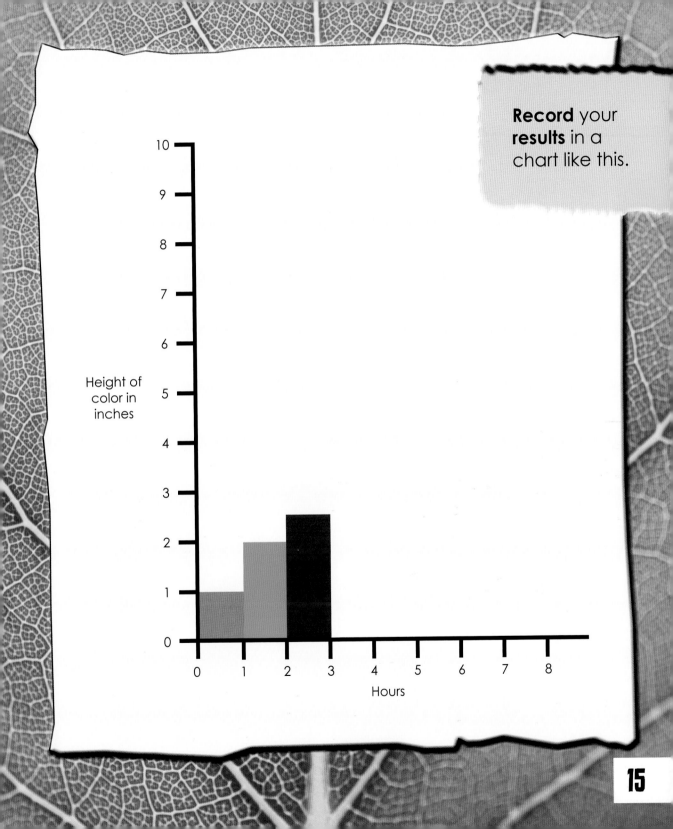

Height of color in inches

Hours

Head for the Sun

Plants need sunlight to grow. Without it, they cannot make the food they need. Some flowers and leaves face east in the morning and then follow the Sun as it moves to the west. Plants growing indoors will often grow toward the nearest light.

Hypothesis

Plants grow best when they have sunlight.

You will need these things for the **experiment**.

Procedure

1. Start with three similar plants. Label them A, B, and C. Put plant A on a sunny window ledge. Put plant B next to an electric lamp. Put plant C in a dark place in the same room.

2. Check the plants every day. Which plant grows the quickest? Which plant grows the slowest? **Record** your **observations**.

Plants make their own food when they take in sunlight.

What would happen to the **stems** if you tipped the pots on their sides? Which way would the stems grow? Which way would the leaves face? Try it. **Record** your **observations**.

You may need to watch for several days to see what happens.

The Science Explained

Plant stems contain special **chemicals**. When light shines on a plant from one side, the chemicals move toward the shaded side of the stem. The chemicals make that side of the plant grow faster. This makes the stem bend toward the light.

Make a Root Viewer

Procedure

1. Cut off the top of a drink carton. Draw a rectangle in the middle of one side. Cut along three sides of the rectangle. Do not cut the bottom side. This will create a "door."

2. Cut a rectangle of plastic wrap. Tape it over the inside of the door to create a window. Use cellophane tape to close the door.

You will need these **materials** for the **experiment**.

3. Half fill the drink carton with potting soil. Add water until the soil is moist.

4. Press **seeds** into the soil. Put the carton on a sunny window ledge. Tilt it toward the window so that the soil can take in sunlight.

5. After the seeds **sprout**, open the door. What can you see? **Record** your **observations**. Close the door again.

Window

You've already seen how leaves and flowers turn toward the Sun. Do **roots** turn toward the Sun, too? Use your root viewer to find out in this **experiment**.

Hypothesis

Plant roots do not grow toward light.

	Day 1	Day 2	Day 3	Day 4	Day 5
Root	≈≈≈	≈≈≈	≈≈≈	≈≈≈	≈≈≈

Write the length in inches of the root in a chart.

Procedure

1. Start after you can see roots. Then tape the door open.
2. Place the viewer so the open side faces the light.
3. Every day, check the root growth. **Record** your **observations** in a chart like the one on page 22.
4. After a week, take the plant out and lay it on some newspaper. (Remember which side was near the light!)
5. Gently brush soil from the roots. Which side has more root growth?

The Science Explained

Roots take in **chemicals** and water from the soil. They work best in the dark, growing away from the light.

Open and Shut Case!

A closed pinecone on a tree contains **seeds**. The pinecone needs to open so the seeds can fall out. The best time for this to happen is in dry weather when the seeds are more likely to blow away from the parent tree. When the pinecones get wet, they close up again.

Hypothesis

A pinecone opens when it is dry and closes when it is wet, even if it isn't on a tree.

You will need these things for the **experiment**.

Procedure

1. Place some pinecones in a plastic bag. Fill the bag with water. Seal the bag.

2. Wait for 15 minutes. What has happened to the pinecones? Compare one of these wet pinecones to a dry pinecone. How is a wet pinecone different? **Record** your **observations**.

3. Take your wet pinecones out of the bag. Shake off any extra water. Put them on a cake pan. Ask an adult to put the cake pan in an oven heated to the coolest setting. Wait for 30 minutes. Has the pinecone changed again? Look again after one hour.

Warning!

Always use oven mitts to hold a hot cake pan.

4. Take the pinecones out of the oven. Let them sit overnight. Compare them to the dry pinecone. Draw pictures in your **log**. How many days does it take before they look like the dry pinecone?

Which pinecone looks like the pinecones that were in the oven?

Your Turn!

Plants are important for many reasons. They help clean the air. They make **oxygen**, which humans and other animals need to breathe.

What would happen if there was no sunlight? Could we grow plants using another kind of light? Think about what you have learned. How could you find out? Design an **experiment** to test your idea.

Glossary

botanist scientist who studies plants

chemical substance made of certain materials

conclusion what you learn from the results of an experiment

data information gathered in an experiment

experiment organized way of testing an idea

hypothesis suggested statement or explanation that can be tested

log written notes about an experiment

materials anything used for making something else

observation something you notice, or observe, with any of your five senses

observe watch, or notice, something

oxygen gas in the air. Humans and animals need oxygen to breathe.

procedure steps followed to carry out an experiment

record draw or write something down

results what happens in an experiment

root underground part of a plant. Plants take in water in the soil through their roots.

seed part of a plant that is made by flowers that can grow into a new plant

sprout grow

stem part of a plant that holds up the leaves and flowers

Find Out More

Books

Kim, Sue. *How Does A Seed Grow?* New York: Little Simon, 2010.

Parker, Vic. *How Big is Big? Comparing Plants.* Chicago: Heinemann, 2010.

Schuh, Mari. *All Kinds of Gardens.* Mankato, Minn.: Capstone, 2010.

Websites

Agriculture Research Project's Sci4Kids
www.ars.usda.gov/is/kids/

Science Kids: How Plants Grow
www.sciencekids.co.nz/gamesactivities/plantsgrow.html

Wonderville—Discover the fun of science
www.wonderville.ca/browse/activities

Index